Beginnings

N O T E S

Canadian representatives: General Publishing Co., Ltd.,
30 Lesmill Road, Don Mills, Ontario M3B 2T6.

9 8 7 6 5 4 3 2 1
Digit on the right indicates the number of this printing.

ISBN 1-56138-579-4

Cover design by Toby Schmidt
Cover and interior illustrations by Valerie Coursen
Interior design by Susan E. Van Horn
Edited by Brian Perrin
Typography by Justin T. Scott
Printed in the United States

This book may be ordered by mail from the publisher.
Please add $1.00 for postage and handling.
But try your bookstore first!

Running Press Book Publishers
125 South Twenty-second Street
Philadelphia, Pennsylvania 19103-4399

Beginnings

NOTES

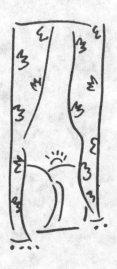

RUNNING PRESS
PHILADELPHIA · LONDON

When shall we live, if not now?

Lucius Annaeus Seneca (c. 4 B.C.–65 A.D.)
Roman philosopher and statesman

36 B
37 C
38 B
39 C
40 D
41 D
42 A
43
44
45
46
47
48 A
49
50

51
52
53
54
55
56
57
58
59
60
61
62
63
64
65
66
67
68
69
70

21

49

1/ A. ✓	17/ D. ✓	35, D. ✓	56, D. ✓
2/ B. ✓	18/ A. ✓	36, C ✗	57, B. ✓
3/ A ✗	19/ A. ✓	37, C ✓	58, C. ✗
4/ B. ✓	20/ C. ✓	38, B ✓	59, B. ✓
5/ C. ✗	21/ A. ✗	39, C ✓	60, A. ✓
6/ A. ✓	22, C. ✗	40, A ✗	61, B. ✓
7/ D. ✓	23, C. ✓	41, B ✓	62, D ✓
8/ A. ✓	24, B ✓	42, A ✓	63, D. ✓
9/ D. ✓	25, A ✗	43, B. ✓	64, B. ✓
10, B ✓	26, A. ✓	44, D ✓	65, C. ✓
11, D. ✗	27, C. ✓	45, D ✗	66, D. ✗
12, B. ✓	28, B ✗	46, B ✓	67, A. ✗
13, A. ✓	29, D ✗	47, D. ✓	68, A. ✗
14, B. ✓	30, C. ✓	48, C ✗	69, A. ✓
15, C. ✓	31, A. ✓	49, D ✓	70, A. ✗
16, D. ✓	32, C ✗	50, C ✓	
	33, C. ✓	51, A ✗	
	34, B ✓	52, A ✗	
		53, B. ✓	
		54, A ✗	
		55, A. ✓	

49

109*

Where there is an open mind, there will always be a frontier.

CHARLES F. KETTERING (1876–1958)
AMERICAN ENGINEER

The great majority of men are bundles of beginnings.

Ralph Waldo Emerson (1803–1882)
American poet and writer

*L*ife consists of propositions about life.

Wallace Stevens (1879–1955)
American poet

. . . human beings are not born once and for all on the day

their mothers give birth to them, but . . . life obliges them

over and over again to give birth to themselves.

Gabriel García Márquez (b. 1928)
Colombian writer

To exist is to change; to change is to mature;

to mature is to create oneself endlessly.

HENRI BERGSON (1859–1941)
FRENCH PHILOSOPHER AND PSYCHOLOGIST

There's nothing in a caterpillar that tells you it's going to be a
butterfly. Who knows what man *can become?*

R. Buckminster Fuller (1895–1983)
American architect and inventor

Life is for delving, discovering, learning.

Louis L'Amour (1908–1988)
American writer

. . . growth comes from saying yes to the unknown.

Life can only be understood backwards.

It must be lived forwards.

Søren Kierkegaard (1813–1855)
Danish philosopher

*L*ife never presents us with anything
which may not be looked upon as a
fresh starting point, no less than
as a termination.

ANDRÉ GIDE (1869–1951)
FRENCH WRITER

Now is not the time to cling to what was,

but to amend what is.

Helen Hayes (1900–1993)
American actress

The present was an egg laid by the past that had the future inside its shell.

Zora Neale Hurston (1902–1960)
American writer

The future is purchased by the present.

SAMUEL JOHNSON (1709–1784)
ENGLISH POET AND WRITER

Where there is hope there is life,

where there is life there is

possibility and where there is

possibility change can occur.

Jesse Jackson (b. 1941)
American cleric, politician,
and civil rights leader

$\mathcal{W}$here to start is the problem, because nothing begins when it begins and nothing's over when it's over, and everything needs a preface: a preface, a postscript, a chart of simultaneous events.

MARGARET ATWOOD (B. 1939)
CANADIAN WRITER

The world is round and the place which may seem like the end may also be only the beginning.

Ivy Baker Priest (1905–1975)
United States Treasurer

*W*hen you understood the great round, then you could change things, even after they happened, because every chance came again, if you recognized it.

Elizabeth Cunningham (b. 1953)
American writer

We need to remember that we are
created creative and can invent new
scenarios as frequently as they
are needed.

MAYA ANGELOU (B. 1928)
AMERICAN WRITER

Only the first swath cut by the scythe is difficult.

Aleksandr Solzhenitsyn (b. 1918)
Russian writer

I intend to stake out my own claim, a tiny one, but my own.

Henry Miller (1891–1980)
American writer

. . . there is no abdicating to another
captain. We can only chart the
situation, and sail.

RICHARD POWERS (B. 1957)
AMERICAN WRITER

I believe that the direction of
our lives is more important than the
speed at which we travel them.

Harriet Goldhor Learner
Contemporary American psychologist and writer

I am where I am because I believe in all possibilities.

Whoopi Goldberg (b. 1950)
American entertainer

Imagination is everything, . . . It is the
preview of life's coming attractions.

ALBERT EINSTEIN (1879–1955)
GERMAN-BORN AMERICAN PHYSICIST

*Y*ou can be reborn every
day if you live your life as a
smart cookie.

Sonya Friedman (b. 1936)
American psychologist, television
personality, and writer

It's all what you make of it. . . . the possibilities are endless.

Ridley Pearson (b. 1953)
American writer

*T*he spirit knows that its growth is the real aim of existence.

SAUL BELLOW (B. 1915)
CANADIAN-BORN AMERICAN WRITER

Growing is the reward of learning.

Malcolm X (1925–1965)
American activist and writer

*I*f we begin with certainties, we shall end in doubts; but if we begin with doubts, and are patient in them, we shall end in certainties.

Francis Bacon (1561–1626)
English lawyer, philosopher, and writer

. . . it's never too late to start a new life of learning.

PETER HOEG (B. 1957)
DANISH WRITER

*Use missteps as stepping stones
to deeper understanding and
greater achievement.*

Susan Taylor (b. 1946)
American editor

Never take a step backward, not even to gain momentum.

Andy Garcia (b. 1956)
Cuban-born American actor

If you are going to break a rule, capitalize on it. Do it big. Exploit it. Turn it into a virtue.

ROGER ZELAZNY
CONTEMPORARY AMERICAN WRITER

I was taught to learn who you were, who you are,

and who you're going to be.

Nathan Lee Chasing His Horse
Contemporary Native American (Lakota Sioux) actor

*K*now whence you came. If you know whence you came, there is really no limit to where you can go.

James Baldwin (1924–1987)
American playwright and writer